T0196755

THE ANOINTING

GEORGE MOORE

iUniverse, Inc.
New York Bloomington

The Anointing

iUniverse books may be ordered through booksellers or by contacting:

iUniverse
1663 Liberty Drive
Bloomington, IN 47403
www.iuniverse.com
1-800-Authors (1-800-288-4677)

ISBN: 978-1-4401-1851-7 (sc)
ISBN: 978-1-4401-1852-4 (ebook)

Printed in the United States of America

iUniverse rev. date: 03/10/09

For my wife

Christine Moore

Thank you for taking

care of me

To God be the glory.

The anointing has no impossibilities,

just possibilities

George Moore

TABLE OF CONTENTS

CHAPTER 1

The Anointing

The anointing is simply the tangible power of God. It is worthwhile experiencing it. When you experience it, you will never be the same again. The anointing changes men, empowers them to move in the power of God to perform the supernatural. The anointing is a supernatural enablement offered by God to men for His service.

I was born again in July, 1985 and started praying for the Lord to fill me with His precious Holy Spirit. In December of the same year while working at my job, I suddenly found myself speaking with other tongues. I spoke in tongues the whole day. Shortly, afterward the doors began to open for me to preach the gospel. As I began preaching the gospel, I experienced a supernatural enablement. I spoke with power and authority. I had been anointed. Since that time, the anointing of God has been upon my life. I am able to work for God to be His representative because of the anointing. Without the anointing, I will be alone and not effective, but with it, effectiveness will color my whole endeavor.

I stated above that when the Holy Spirit came upon me, I spoke with other tongues. Speaking with other tongues is a supernatural enablement given by the Holy Spirit. The Bible definitely documents that when one is filled with the Holy Spirit, the initial evidence is speaking with other tongues.

"Now when the Day of Pentecost had fully come, they were all with one accord in one place. And suddenly there came a sound from heaven, as of a rushing mighty wind, and it filled the whole house where they were sitting. Then they were all filled with the Holy Spirit, and began to speak with other tongues, as the Spirit gave them utterance" (Acts 2:1-4). Here, we see that, when they were filled with the Holy Spirit, they spoke with other tongues.

"While Peter was still speaking these words, the Holy Spirit fell upon all those who heard the word. And those of the circumcision who believed were astonished, as many as came with Peter because the gift of the Holy Spirit had been poured on the Gentiles also. For they heard them speak with tongues and magnify God. Then Peter answered, 'Can anyone forbid water, that these should not be baptized who have received the Holy Spirit just as we have?' And he commanded them to be baptized in the name of the Lord. Then they asked him to stay a few days" (Acts 10:44-46). Here, again when they were filled with the Holy Spirit, they spoke with tongues.

"And it happened, while Apollos was at Corinth, that Paul, having passed through the upper regions, came to Ephesus. And finding some disciples, he said to them, 'Did you receive the Holy Spirit when you believed?' And they said to him, 'We have not so much as heard whether there is a Holy Spirit.' and he said to them, 'Into what then were you baptized?' So they said, 'Into John's baptism.' Then Paul said, 'John indeed baptized with a baptism of repentance, saying to the people that they should believe on Him who would come after him, that is. on Christ Jesus.' When they heard this, they were baptized in the name of the Lord Jesus Christ. And when Paul had laid hands on them, the Holy Spirit came upon them, and they spoke with tongues and prophesied. Now the men were about twelve in all" (Acts 19:1-7). Here, again we see that when the men were filled with the Holy Spirit, they spoke with other tongues.

Jesus spoke that those who believe in Him will speak with other tongues. "And these signs will follow those who believe. In My name they will cast out demons; they will speak with new tongues" (Mark 16:17). Those who have received the Holy Spirit are those who believe in Jesus Christ.

Let us take the time to study more on the anointing, and various aspects of it.

The anointing, which is pouring oil upon, was performed upon:

a. The patriarchs.

  1 Chr. 16:15-27, 31, 22, "The covenant which He made with Abraham, and His oath to Isaac. And confirmed it to Jacob for a statue, to Israel for an everlasting covenant" vs. 21, "He permitted no man to do them wrong. Yes, He reproved Kings for their sakes" vs. 22, saying, "Do not touch My anointed ones, and do My prophets no harm."

b. Priest

  Ex. 29:1, 7, "And this is what you shall do to them to hallow them for ministering to Me as priests. Take one young bull and two rams without blemish" vs. 7 "And you shall take the anointing oil, pour it on his head, and anoint him."

c. Prophets.

  1 King 19:16, "And you shall anoint Jehu the son of Nimshi as king over Israel. And Elisha the son of Shaphat of Abel Meholal you shall anoint as prophet in your place."

d.   Israel's kings.

       1 Sam 10:1, "Then Samuel took a flask of oil and poured it on his head, and kissed him and said, 'Is it not because the LORD has anointed you commander over His inheritance?'"

e.   Foreign kings.

       1 Kin 19:15, "Then the LORD said to him, 'Go, return on your way to the Wilderness of Damascus; and when you arrive, anoint Hazael as King over Syria.'"

f.   The Messianic King.

       Ps. 2:2, "The kings of the earth set themselves, and the rulers take counsel together, against the LORD and against His Anointed."

g.   Sacred objects.

       Ex. 30:26-28, "With it you shall anoint the tabernacle of meeting and the ark of the Testimony; the table and all its utensils, the lampstand and its utensils, and the altar of incense."

The ordinary purposes of the anointing are:

a.   Adornment.

       Ruth 3:3, "Therefore wash yourself and anoint yourself, put on your best garment and go down to the threshing floor; but do not make yourself known to the man until he has finished eating and drinking."

b.   Invigoration.

       2 Sam 12:20 "So David arose from the ground, washed and anointed himself, and changed his clothes; and he went into the house of the LORD and worshiped. Then he went to his own house, and when he requested, they set food before him, and he ate."

c.   Hospitality.

Luke 7:38, 46, "And stood at His feet behind Him weeping; and she began to wash his feet with her tears, and wiped them with the hair of her head; and she kissed His feet and anointed them with the fragrant oil."

d.   Battle.

Is. 21:5, "Prepare the table. Set a watchman in the tower. Eat and drink. Arise, you princes, anoint the shield."

e.   Burial.

Matt. 26:12, "For in pouring this fragrant oil on My body, she did it for My burial."

f.   Sanctifying.

Ex. 30:29, "You shall sanctify them, that they may be most holy; whatever touches them must be holy."

The following are the medicinal purposes of the anointing:

a.   Wound.

Luke 10:34, "And went to him and bandaged his wounds, pouring on oil and wine; and he set him on his own animal, brought him to an inn, and took care of him."

b.   Healing.

Mark 6:13, "And they cast out many demons, and anointed with oil many who were sick and healed them."

James 5:14, "Is anyone among you sick? Let him cal for the elders of the church, and let them pray over him, anointing him with oil in the name of the Lord."

The following are the sacred purposes of the anointing:

a.   Memorialize an event.

Gen. 28:18, "Then Jacob rose early in the morning, and took the stone that he had put at his head, set it up as a pillar, and poured oil on top of it."

b.   Confirm a covenant.

Gen. 35:14, "So Jacob set up a pillar in the place where He talked with him, a pillar of stone and he poured a drink offering on it, and he poured oil on it.

c.   Set apart.

Ex. 30:22-29, "Moreover the LORD spoke to Moses, saying: 'Also take for yourself quality spices, five hundred shekels of liquid, myrrh half as much sweet-smelling cinnamon (two hundred and fifty shekels), two hundred and fifty shekels of sweet smelling cane, five hundred shekels of cassia, according to the shekel of the sanctifying, and a hint of olive oil. And you shall make from these a holy anointing oil, an ointment compounded according to the art of the perfumer. It shall be a holy anointing oil. With it you shall anoint the tabernacle of meeting and the ark of the Testimony, the table and all its utensils, the lampstand and its utensils, and the altar of incense, the altar of burnt offering with all its utensils, and the laver and its base. You shall sanctify them, that they may be most holy. Whatever touches them must be holy."

d.   Institute into office.

1 Sam. 16:12, 13, "So he sent and brought him in. Now he was ruddy with bright eyes, and good-looking. And the LORD said, 'Arise, anoint him, for this is the one!' Then Samuel took the horn of oil and anointed him in the midst of his brothers, and the Spirit of the LORD

came upon David from that day forward. So Samuel arose and went to Ramah."

Absence of the anointing:

a. Sign of judgment.

    Deut. 28:40, "You shall have olive trees throughout all their territory, but you shall not anoint yourself with the oil, for your olives shall drop off."

b. Fasting.

    2 Sam. 12:16, 20, "David, therefore pleaded with God for the child, and David fasted and went in and lay all night on the ground," vs. 20. "So David arose from the ground, washed and anointed himself, and changed his clothes, and he went into the house of the LORD and worshipped. then he went to his own house; and when he requested, they set food before him, and he ate."

c. Mourning.

    2 Sam. 14:2, "And Joab sent to Tekoa and brought from there a wise woman, and said to her, 'Please pretend to be a mourner, and put on mourning apparel; do not anoint yourself with oil, but act like a woman who has been mourning a long time for the dead.'"

The anointing on Christ the Messiah, the anointed one is as follows:

a. Predicted.

    Ps. 45:7, "You love righteousness and hate wickedness, therefore God, Your God has anointed You with the oil of gladness more than Your companions."

b. Fulfilled.

    Luke 4:18, "The Spirit of the LORD is upon Me, Because He has anointed Me to preach the gospel to the poor. He has sent Me to heal the brokenhearted, to preach deliverance to the captives and recovery of sight to the blind. To set at liberty those who are oppressed. To preach the acceptable year of the LORD."

c. Interpreted.

Act 4:37, "For truly against Your holy Servant Jesus, whom You anointed, both Herod and Pontius Pilate, with the Gentiles and the people of Israel, were gathered together."

d. Symbolized in His name ("the Christ").

Matt. 16:16, 20, "And Simon Peter answered and said, 'You are the Christ, the Son of the living God'" vs. 20. "Then He commanded His disciples that they should tell no one that He was Jesus the Christ."

e. Typical of the believer's anointing.

1 John 2:27, "But the anointing which you have received from Him abides in you, and you do not need that anyone teach you; but as the same anointing teaches you concerning all things, and is true, and is not a lie and just as it has taught you, you will abide in Him."

It is worth a mention to make some notations from this verse of the scriptures.

1. The anointing comes from the Lord.

Our anointing comes from the Lord. Jesus is the baptizer in the Holy Spirit. He has anointed us for His service. While on earth, He told His disciples that when He leaves, the comforter will come. When He left, on the day of Pentecost, the Holy Spirit descended upon men, thus the anointing came down on men. The disciples went from there and did great things for the Lord. Our anointing comes from Him, that should inspire us to go forward and accomplish great things for the Lord. You look at the anointing on Jesus, and it must inspire us to do greater deeds for God. The anointing on Christ made Him do extraordinary miracles and perform great deeds for God, our anointing coming from Him should therefore produce similar results.

2.   The anointing abides in us.

The Christian must realize that they carry with them wherever they go the anointing. The abiding anointing has therefore a mighty purpose. Visualize the anointed, in a world of chaos, carrying an anointing that helps humanity solve its aches. Let the anointing abiding in you, produce mighty results for God.

3.   The anointing will teach you.

The Bible says that "the Spirit will lead you into all truth" (John 16:13). The Spirit of God is all-knowing. He can explain and guide you into every truth.

"Eye has not seen, nor ear heard, nor have entered into the heart of man, the things which God has prepared for those who love Him. But God has revealed them to us through His Spirit. For the Spirit searches all things, yes, the deep things of God" (1 Cor. 2:10).

"But I make known to you, brethren, that the gospel which was preached by me is not according to man. For I neither received it from man, nor was I taught it; but it came through the revelation of Jesus Christ" (Gal. 1:11-12).

"...Surely I will pour out my spirit on you; I will make my words known to you" (Prov. 1:23). When the Spirit of God is poured out on an individual, he is placed at a position where God's word becomes known to him.

4.   The anointing is true.

The word true means actual, authentic, accurate, correct, exact, constant, honest, faithful, loyal, reliable, valid, legitimate, steadfast, sincere.

The anointing is actual. It is the actual power of God. It is what God has given His children for His service.

The anointing is authentic. It is the power of God. You can rest your absolute faith in it. The anointing is accurate. The anointing in its summation purely comes from the Holy God.

The anointing is correct. In this world, there are wrong and correct aspects. The anointing is a component that descends from the Lord of Hosts and correct, in other words, right in every sense. The anointing is exact. the anointing is the exact power of God.

The anointing is genuine. When you have God's power in your life, you are carrying an enormous commodity, precious in every way, and comes directly from the mighty God. The anointing is real. The anointing remains the greatest reality you can encounter. You can feel His touch.

The anointing is veracious. You can trust in the power of God.

The anointing is veritable. Have faith in God.

The anointing is constant. The anointing abides in us.

The anointing is honest. God is an honest God; so is His power.

The anointing is faithful. The anointing will do what God has sent it to do.

The anointing is loyal. You can depend on God's mighty anointing.

The anointing is reliable. If you can rely on anyone, you can definitely do so with God.

The anointing is valid. Believe in the power of our God.
The anointing is legitimate. God is the One true God. Trust in Him.
The anointing is steadfast. Trust in the Lord completely.
The anointing is sincere. What an awesome and precious God. Thank you for your power.
The anointing can be felt. You can experience the power of the anointing. People have felt the anointing on my life and made remarkable comments. People have been slain in the Spirit, cried, shouted, applauded, wept, expressed joy or other positive emotions when they felt the anointing.
The truth of the anointing is validated by the results it produces.
Miracles, signs and wonders are common outcomes of the anointing.

5. The anointing is not a lie.

The word lie means untruth, fib, illusion, delusion, falsehood, fiction, equivocation, prevarication, repose, locution, perjury, misinform, site, recline, similitude.
The anointing is none of the above. The anointing is real and truth. The anointing will point you to the truth. The anointing is not a lie, so be reassured that with it, you will be productive in the service of the master. With the anointing, you have a power that comes from the Spirit of truth.
The anointing is not a lie in terms of the fact that, it has nothing but truth in its makeup, and only that ingredient is available in its output.

6. You do not need that anyone teach you.

This is indeed a very puzzling statement and many may find difficulty in truly dissecting it. The Spirit shed light on the subject for me. It means it does not matter who is preaching or teaching, it is the anointing that will make spiritual truths available to you. The anointing teaches you.

The following are the significance of the anointing:

a. Divine appointment.

2 Chr. 22:7, "His going to Joram was God's occasion for Ahaziah's downfall, for when he arrived, he went out with Jehroam against Jehu, the son of Nimshi, whom the LORD had anointed to cut off the house of Ahab."

b. Special honor.

1 Sam. 24:6, 10, "And he said to his men, 'The LORD forbid that I should do this thing to my master, the LORD's anointed, to stretch out my hand against him, seeing he is the anointed of the LORD'" vs. 10, "Look, this day your eyes have seen that the LORD delivered you today into my hand in the cave, and someone urged me to kill, but my eye spared you, and I said, 'I will not stretch out my hand against my Lord, for he is the Lord's anointed.'"

c. Special privilege.

Ps. 105:15, "Do not touch My anointed ones, and do My prophets no harm."

CHAPTER 2

The Holy Spirit

"And it happened, while Apollos was at Corinth, that Paul, having passed through the upper regions, came to Ephesus. And finding some disciples, he said to them, 'Did you receive the Holy Spirit when you believed?' And they said to him, 'We have not so much as heard whether there is a Holy Spirit?' And he said to them, 'Into what then were you baptized?' So they said, 'Into John's baptism.' Then Paul said, 'John indeed baptized with a baptism of repentance, saying to the people that they should believe on Him who would come after him, that is, on Christ Jesus.' When they heard this, they were baptized in the name of the Lord Jesus Christ. And when Paul had laid hands on them, the Holy Spirit came upon them, and they spoke with tongues and prophesied. Now the men were about twelve in all" (Acts 19:1-7).

In the above scripture, Paul meets some disciples and asked them if they had received the Holy Spirit. They declared they do not know of the Holy Spirit. Reading this scripture, I felt strongly to write about the Holy Spirit and hopefully educate some readers that may possibly be in the same sphere these believers at Ephesus were. Also it is of supreme essence to know more about the Holy Spirit because He has everything to do with the anointing.

The Holy Spirit is the third person of the Godhead, and possesses a mighty and wonderful ministry in the body of Christ. The Holy Spirit is a person and His ministry in the believer's life is unmeasureable and of supreme importance. One of the most serious errors in the minds of many people concerning the Holy Spirit is that He is simply a principle or an influence. On the contrary, the Holy Spirit is as much a person as the Father and the Son.

In the scriptures, there are several titles which are applied to the Holy Spirit:
In Genesis 1:2, He is called "The Spirit of God."
In Isaiah 61:1, He is called "The Spirit of the Father."
In Zechariah 12:10, He is called "The Spirit of Truth."
In Romans 1:4, He is called "The Spirit of Holiness"
In Romans 8:2, He is called, "the Spirit of life."
In Romans 8:9, He is called, "The Spirit of Adoption."
In 1 Peter 4:14, He is called, "The Spirit of Glory."
In Rev. 9:10, He is called "the Spirit of Prophecy."
In Gen. 6:3, He is called "My Spirit."
In Psalm 51:11, He is called "Holy Spirit."
All these names attributed to the Holy Spirit has to do with a quality or an area of activity by Him.

The Holy Spirit is omnipotent. Luke 4:34-36 reads, "Then Mary said to the angel, 'How can this be, since I do not know a man?' And the angel said to her, 'The Holy Spirit will come upon you and the power of the Highest will overshadow you. Therefore, also, the Holy One who is to be born will be called the Son of God.'" The Holy Spirit possesses the power of the Highest. His power is unlimited. He is omnipotent.

The Holy Spirit is omniscient; literally meaning He is all-knowing. 1 Corinthians 2:10-11 reads, "But God has revealed them to us through His Spirit. For the Spirit searches all things, yes the deep things of God. For what man knows the thing of a man except the spirit of man which is in him? Even so, no man knows the things of God except the God." The Holy Spirit being omniscient means that He knows everything about everybody. He is aware of the storms, pains, hurts and struggles that human beings encounter and being God, He is able to help us.

The Holy Spirit is omnipresent. Psalm 139:7-13 reads: "Where can I go from your Spirit? Or where can I flee from your presence? If I ascend to heaven, You are there. If I make my bed in hell, behold, you are there. If I take the wings of the morning and dwell in the uttermost parts of the sea, even there Your hand shall lead us, and Your right hand shall hold me. If I shall say, surely the darkness shall fall on me, even the night shall be light about me; indeed, the darkness shall not hide from You, but the night shines as the day, the darkness and the light are both alike to You. For you have formed my inward parts You have covered me in my mother's womb."

Psalm 139:7 reads, "Where can I go from your Spirit," or where can I flee from Your presence? The answer is practically nowhere. The Holy Spirit is God, and because of that, He is aware of wherever we are at any time, and wherever we choose to go, He is aware.

The Holy Spirit being a person, possesses a personality. The Bible speaks of the mind of the Holy Spirit. Romans 8:27, reads, "Now He who searches the hearts know what the mind of the Spirit is, because He makes intercession for the saints according to the will of God." The Bible also speaks of the will of the Holy Spirit. 1 Corinthians 12:11 says, "But one and the same Spirit works all these things, distributing to each individually as He wills.

In the book of Acts, the Holy Spirit is often described as speaking directly to men. During Paul's second missionary journey, the apostle was forbidden by the spirit to visit another field of service (Acts 16:6, 7); and then he was instructed to proceed toward a different field of service (Acts 16:10).

It was God's Spirit who spoke directly to Christian leaders, in the Antioch Church, commanding them to send Paul and Barnabas on their first missionary journey (Acts 13:2). Today the Holy Spirit is speaking through anointed and chosen men and women of God, and generally through all Christians. Bless the Holy Name of the Holy Spirit.

Another aspect which clearly states that the Holy Spirit possesses a personality is that He teaches. John 14:26 reads, "But the Helper, the Holy Spirit, whom the Father will send in My name, He will teach you all things, and bring to your remembrance all things that I have said to you." Jesus was speaking to His disciples and also to us that, the Holy Spirit will teach us concerning all the things that He speaks which at times are hard to understand. However, in the broader picture, Jesus was telling us that, the Holy Spirit will teach us concerning the things of God. The teaching that the Holy Spirit has given to Christians and the church in general has definitely been tremendous and has been the key to the growth of Christians and the development and advancement of the ministry of Christ on earth.

Another aspect of the personality of the Holy Spirit is that He strives with sinners—Genesis 6:3 reads, "My Spirit shall not always strive with man." The Holy Spirit convicts the sinner of his sin and draws him to repentance in Christ Jesus. However, there can be a case where the Holy Spirit will keep convicting a person for a mighty long time, and the person never repents. The person's heart can be hardened, and the spirit will not continue to strive with that person, which definitely means that the Holy Spirit will not continue to convict the person. This is a very dangerous situation since without the conviction of the Holy Spirit, no one can be saved.

Another aspect of the personality of the Holy Spirit is that He helps our weaknesses. Romans 8:26 reads: "Likewise the

Spirit also helps in our weaknesses. For we do not know what we should pray for as we ought but the Spirit makes intercession for us with groanings which cannot be uttered."

The Holy Spirit is grieved. Acts 4:30 reads, "And do not grieve the Holy Spirit of God, by whom you were sealed for the day of redemption."

The Holy Spirit is resisted. Acts 7:31 reads, "You stiffnecked and uncircumcised in heart and ears. You always resist the Holy Spirit; as your fathers did, so do you."

The ministry of Jesus Christ was totally under the anointing of the Holy Spirit. Luke 4:14 reads, "Then Jesus returned in the power of the Spirit to Galilee, and news of Him went out through all the surrounding region." Luke 4:18 reads, "The Spirit of the Lord is upon Me, because He has anointed Me to preach the gospel to the poor. He has sent Me to heal the broken-hearted. To preach deliverance to the captives, and recovery of sight to the blind, to set at liberty those who are oppressed, and to preach the acceptable year of the Lord." Jesus totally depended upon the Spirit of God to preach and teach, and He had enormous success in His ministry.

God did tremendous miracles through Jesus by the power of the Holy Spirit. Luke 11:20 reads, "But if I cast out demons by the Spirit of God, surely the kingdom of God has come upon you."

The miracles that Jesus performed were two kinds. Those that He performed on man, and those that He performed in the sphere of external nature. Examples of the miracles He performed on man included: the man with the unclean spirit in the synagogue who was cured (Mark 1:23-26); the centurion's servant who was cured of palsy (Matthew 8:5-13); Lazarus who was raised from the dead (John 11:38-44); the woman with the issue of blood who was healed (Matthew 9:20-22); the withered hand which was restored (Luke 6:6-11); and the blind man who was healed (Mark 8:22-26). Examples of miracles performed in the sphere of external nature include Jesus and Peter walking on the sea (Matthew 14:25-33) and the windstorm that was stilled (Matthew 8:23-27).

The power of the Holy Spirit resurrected Jesus Christ from the dead. Romans 1:4 reads, "...and declared to be the son of God, according to the Spirit of holiness, by the resurrection from the dead." When Jesus was crucified and laid to rest, His disciples, although He had told them He was going to be resurrected, doubted about it. However, the Holy Spirit is omnipotent; there is no limit to His power. He can raise the dead; He can heal any sickness or disease; He can set the captives free; and He performs miracles.

The greatest miracle is the salvation of a soul, and the Holy Spirit plays a significant role in ensuring the occurrence of it.

There are three wonderful works performed by the Holy Spirit in preparing unsaved people to become Christians.

a. The work of the Holy Spirit in restraining. Satan would enjoy nothing more than to destroy people before they make their decision to accept Christ as savior. But the Holy Spirit prevents this from occurring. Isaiah 59:19 reads, "...when the enemy comes in like a flood, the Spirit of the Lord will lift up a standard against him."

b. The work of the Holy Spirit in convicting. Mankind's sin and righteousness are exposed by the Holy Spirit (John 16:8). Felix, a Roman Governor, actually trembles under conviction as he hears Paul preach (Acts 24:25). The other case involved King Agrippa who responds to a gospel message by saying: "You almost persuaded me to become a Christian" (Acts 26:28).

c. The work of the Holy Spirit in regenerating. When a repenting sinner accepts Jesus as savior he is given a new nature by the Holy Spirit (2 Cor. 5:17). Jesus carefully explained the ministry of the Holy Spirit to Nicodemus (John 3:3-7). (Open Bible, 1240).

The coming of the Holy Spirit was given by the Lord through the prophet Joel (Joel 2:28-32). This prophecy was given by the prophet Joel about eight hundred years before it was fulfilled at Pentecost. Acts, chapter 2, records the earth-changing events of the Day of Pentecsot when the Holy Spirit came. The spirit transforms a small group of fearful men into a thriving, worldwide church that is ever moving forward and fulfilling the Great Commission.

The New Testament writers agree that the giving of the Holy Spirit was withheld after the resurrection and exaltation of Christ, with which events it is intimately connected. But there is no agreement about the manner and the time of the coming of the Spirit. Only two writers describe the original imparting of the Spirit. St. Luke and St. John, and their accounts differ in every particular except that the event took place in Jerusalem. According to St. John, the ascension of the Lord seems to have taken place between the appearance to the disciples the same evening when the doors were shut (John 20:19); at this evening appearance the Risen Jesus imparted the Holy Spirit to the disciples by 'insufflation' (John 20:22). Thus, in St. John's view, the resurrection, the ascension and the giving of the Spirit all seem to have occurred on the same day; this is certainly what we would have inferred from the Fourth Gospel if our minds had not been so familiar with the Lucan version of the events. The evidence of St. Paul, so far as it goes, would seem to agree with the Johannine rather than the Lucan view; Paul does not sharply distinguish between the resurrection or ascension of Christ as separate events, and he certainly regards the appearance of Christ to himself on the Damascus road as being entirely parallel to the appearances to Peter and the other apostles and brethren (1 Cor. 15:5-7), as if they were all (like that to himself) post-ascension appearances of the Lord. (An introduction to the Theology of the New Testament, 116).

There is a work the Holy Spirit does in Christian living. As a loving and wise mother tenderly watches over her child, so the Holy Spirit cares for the children of God.

a.   The Holy Spirit indwells Christians.

       The Bible teaches that all believers are indwelt by the Holy Spirit. First Corinthians 6:19 reads, "Or do you not know that your body is the temple of the Holy Spirit who is in you, whom you have from God, and you are not your own." The purpose of this indwelling ministry is to control the newly nature given at conversion (2 Cor. 5:17).

b.   The Holy Spirit fills believers.

c.   The Holy Spirit sanctifies the believer. Rom. 15:16 reads, "…that I might be a minister of Jesus Christ to the Gentiles ministering the gospel of God, that the offerings of the Gentiles might be acceptable, sanctified by the Holy Spirit." 2 Thessalonians 2:13 reads, "But we are bound by the Lord, because God from the beginning chose you for salvation through sanctification by the Spirit and belief in the truths."

d.   The Holy Spirit produces fruit in the life of the believer. This fruit is described by Paul: "But the fruit of the Spirit is love, joy, peace, longsuffering, kindness, goodness, faithfulness, gentleness, self-control (Galatians 5:22, 23).

e.   The Holy Spirit imparts gifts to Christians (Romans 12:6-8, 1 Corinthians 12:1-11).

The Holy Spirit has a very wonderful ministry in the church. Not only does He fill and baptize believers, but He does the following as well:

a.   He appoints officers.

"Therefore take heed to yourself and to all the flock, among which the Holy Spirit had made you overseers, to shepherd the church of God which He purchased with His own blood (Acts 20:28).

b.   He sends out missionaries.

"As they ministered to the Lord and fasted, the Holy Spirit said, "Now separate for Me Barnabas and Saul for the work to which I have called them" (Acts 13:2). "So, being sent out by the Holy Spirit, they went down to Selecia, and from there they sailed to Cyrus" (Acts 13:4).

c.   He directs missionaries.

"Then the Holy Spirit said to Phillip, 'Go near and overtake the chariot'" (Acts 8:29).

d.   He comforts the church.

"Then the churches throughout all Judea, Galilee and Samaria had peace and were edified. And walking in the fear of the Lord and in the comfort of the Holy Spirit, they were multiplied" (Acts 9:31).

e.   The Holy Spirit empowers.

"But truly I am full of power by the Spirit of the Lord, and of justice and might, to declare to Jacob his transgression and to Israel his sin" (Micah 3:8).

The Holy Spirit helps the believer to pray. The Holy Spirit is the spirit of prayer. He prays directly, speaking with the Father and the Son. He also prays indirectly praying through you, the believer. It is the nature of God the Son and God the Spirit to pray. They ever live to pray. Just as God has ordained that you join Christ in intercession for His will to be done on earth, so He has ordained that the Holy Spirit should enable, guide and empower your intercession.

To say it in another startling way: God the Son is your enthroned Prayer Partner. Just as God the Father remains invisible to your human eyes, so God the Spirit remains invisible. But just as surely as you can know the Fatherhood of God and the saviorhood of Christ, even so you can know when the Holy Spirit is working within you. To be filled with the Spirit is to be with the spirit of intercession.

When the Holy Spirit fills, prayer becomes your very spiritual breath. The Holy Spirit loves to do within you that for which He indwells you—to accomplish God's will on earth. God has ordained that the prayer of the believer, is one of the major ways He accomplishes His will, so the Holy Spirit desires to make intercession a major expression of your spiritual life.

The Holy Spirit enables and transforms your prayer. There are a number of aspects concerning the ministry of the Holy Spirit in this area that I will like to introduce.

1.   The Holy Spirit increases your desire to pray. Just as it is natural for a child to talk to his father, so it is natural for the believer to pray to the heavenly Father. Though a child must learn to talk, a new believer can pray as soon as he is of the Spirit, born again. The Holy Spirit is present from the moment of spiritual birth to encourage and increase the desire to pray. It is a sign of spiritual ill health for any Christian to lack this desire. A carnal believer finds many excuses to neglect prayer, for Satan is always ready to try to rob us of communion with God, the source of prayer. But a believer who is Spirit-filled can expect the Holy Spirit, the indwelling prayer Enabler, to draw him to pray.

2.   The Holy Spirit brings scripture to your memory as you pray. One of the ministries of the Spirit, as your Prayer Partner, is to bring to mind the things of spiritual importance. He delights to remind you of verses of scripture, verses filled with praises, so you

can quote them in your prayers. He reminds you of scripture verses to strengthen your faith. Memorizing scripture—hiding in your heart—will enable you to incorporate God's word into your spiritual life (Psalm 119:11). Memorize some of the praise psalms, the doxologies of the New Testament, and some of the verses of the prayer and promise. These can be repeated, for you will find they express the deep desires and the deep joys of your heart. Oh, what a blessing to use God's own words as your prayer.

3. The Holy Spirit brings spiritual goals to your attention. The Spirit loves to place before you the image of Jesus and to deepen your desire to be more like Him as you read about Him in the Word, realizing that you fall short of His Christ-likeness. The Holy Spirit also delights to hold before you Bible characters, outstanding godly people in the history of the church, or people whom you have met or unknown. Using their examples, the Spirit helps you set goals for spiritual growth. There are many passages of the Bible which the Spirit can use in this aspect of His ministry. Therefore, it is very important to spend adequate time reading God's Word systematically day by day. The Spirit will also bring goals to your attention as you pray for your church, your missionary organization, your nation and indeed your world.

4. The Holy Spirit brings needs to your attention. The Holy Spirit can give you eyes to see what others may fail to see. He can help you discern when people are discourages, sad, or defeated. He can point out to your spiritual neglect, the need for revival, for new vision and greater obedience. He can inspire you to pray for the growth of the church, for the youth about you, for specially used servants of God. His bringing of need

to your attention is His call to you to pray. Satan does not object to your recognizing the needs, but he wants you to criticize and ridicule. The Holy Spirit, as your indwelling Prayer Partner, wants to make you prayerful, not critical. Satan wants you to talk about people and their needs, the Holy Spirit wants you to intercede in prayer for them. At times, you should share these concerns with others in order to join in prayer about them, widespread concerns of your community, your nation and your world. The tremendous need for the advance and spread of the gospel calls you to unite in prayer for maximum prayer power. The Holy Spirit is always ready to assist you at such times and Christ promises that He will be present with you (John 14:16).

5. The Holy Spirit places prayer burdens upon you. God's heart is pained by the sin, the indifference, and the godlessness of our age. Our loving Savior and the tender Holy Spirit plead in interceding prayer for the broken homes, and the tragedies of sin and injustice throughout the world. They long for you to join them in daily intercession for the hurting, the broken, the lost, and those destroyed for everyone in need. God hears the cry of the orphan, the sob of the brokenhearted, the angry words of the violent, and the screams of their victims. God feels the woes of the prisoners and the refugees, the hunger pangs of those starving for food. He is touched by the sorrow of those chained by habits of sin. He understands the spiritual darkness and the vague but deep dissatisfaction of those who have never received the gospel. Surely Jesus still weeps over our cities as He wept over Jerusalem, for His heart is the same yesterday, today and forever (Heb. 13:8). He cherishes every human being, no matter how sinful he

is. It is the special role of the Holy Spirit to give you a prayer burden for all these needs and all these needy ones. God wants to express His longing love through you as you pray. Such loving, longing intercession should be a part of your prayer each day. The more faithfully and sincerely you pray for these needs the more deeply the Holy Spirit will be able to burden you with these things which break the heart of God. The Holy Spirit wants to call you to weep with those who weep (Rom 12:15). Your weeping is usually not in public, but in your secret place of intercession (Jer. 13:17).

6.   The Holy Spirit will call you to prayer at crisis moments. There are crisis moments in the lives of all people—moments of danger, moments of decision, moments of special opportunity. There are times when the Holy Spirit is convincing someone of sin (John 16:8), and He may call you to pray during that spiritual crisis. There are times of illness or special discouragement when the Spirit may select you to bear a special prayer burden for someone. Learn to be very sensitive to His voice.

7.   The Holy Spirit will add special depth, power and faith to your prayer. He will not only direct you to pray for special needs, but He will also guide you in how to pray for them, will strengthen your faith as you pray, and will anoint and empower your praying. In addition, as your Prayer Partner, He will join you in praying and interceding at a depth not possible to you alone (Rom. 8:26-27). We are weak in ourselves and our prayers are weak as compared to His. He sees the urgency far better than we do. His infinite personality feels an infinite depth of love, sorrow, compassion and yearning.

He sees the tremendous potential and possibilities beyond anything we could ever understand. The Spirit's prayer, says Paul, transcends any possible prayer on your part. This is not so much His intercession for you (V. 27). He intercedes for you and for those whom you intercede. He has led you to share His heart cry, His burden, His love. But He does not leave you to pray alone. He joins you as your loving Prayer Partner, adding infinite understanding, desire and power.

8. The Holy Spirit wants you to have a worldwide prayer ministry. The Holy Spirit, your indwelling prayer partner longs for you to share His heartbeat for the whole world. Since He is the Creator God, He loves all His creation equally. About half of the people have never heard the name of Jesus, or if they have heard it mentioned, they have not heard enough about Him to enable them to make an intelligent decision to receive Christ. These people live in a kind of poverty not often recognized or publicized. It is a poverty of intercessory prayer, for the intercessors in these heathen nations are few. Who will pray for them? Who will pray for the outcast, the atheist, the communist, the terrorist—if not the Christians in our nation? The Holy Spirit, who prays for them with deep hunger each day, longs for you to share His intercession for the rapid advancement of the gospel. How tragic if our reluctance to pray and our failure to reach these lost ones are factors contributing to the delay of Christ's return. God forgive us.

Why not step right now and ask forgiveness, promising that through the Spirit's enabling power, you will begin to assume your full role as His prayer partner. (Touch the World Through Prayer, 125).

The Holy Spirit is the third person of the Trinity and has a wonderful ministry in the body of Christ. The Trinity cooperates in many aspects concerning the Christian life in general. Although we are interested solely right now on the work and ministry of the Holy Spirit, there is a great work of the Trinity mentioned in the book of Ephesians; but since the Holy Spirit has a part to do with it, I think it is worth mentioning. This work of the Trinity can be divided into three parts.

1. Chose by the Father (Ephesians 1:3-6).

    "Blessed be the God and Father of our Lord Jesus Christ, who has blessed us with every spiritual blessing in the heavenly places in Christ, just as He chose us in Him before the foundation of the world, that we should be holy and without blame before Him in love, having predestined us to adoption as sons by Jesus Christ to Himself according to the good pleasure of His will, to the praise of the glory of His grace, by which He has made us accepted in the Beloved."

2. Redeemed by the Son (Ephesians 1:7-12).

    "In Him we have redemption through His blood, the forgiveness of sins, according to the riches of His grace which He made to abound towards us in all wisdom and prudence, having made known to us the mystery of His will, according to His good pleasure which He purposed in Himself, that is the dispensation of the fullness of the times He might gather together in one all things in Christ, both which are in heaven and which are on earth. In Him, in whom also we have obtained an inheritance, being predestined according to the purpose of Him who works all things according to the counsel of His will, that we who first trusted in Christ should be to the praise of His glory."

3.   Sealed by the Spirit (Ephesians 1:13-14).

In Him you also trusted, after you heard the word of truth, the gospel of your salvation; in whom also, having believed you were sealed with the Holy Spirit of promise, who is the guarantee of our inheritance until the redemption of the purchased possession, to the praise of His glory.

CHAPTER 3
The Presence And The Anointing

There is a distinct difference between the presence of God and the anointing. The former has to do with His tangible presence while the latter specifically His power. In the Old Testament, Prophets, Priests and Kings had dealings with God, in His presence.

Thinking about the presence of God, a number of factor come into play. These factors are not totally exclusive. One could possibly come up with others. the following, however, in my estimation, remain extremely paramount.

1. In His presence is Greatness.

   When you stand in the presence of God, you are in the arena of greatness. 1 Ch. 16:25, "For the LORD is great and greatly to be praised; He is also to be feared above all gods."

   Psalm 104:1, "Bless the LORD, O my soul! O LORD my God, You are very great; You are clothed with honor and majesty."

The Greatness of our God is unmeasurable. It is unending in every sense.

He is the God of Creation. He created all things. Among numerous blessings. He has offered us, He reaches us with enormous help. He saves us. He heals us. He restores us. He is a wonderful Father who cares. He is a Great God. He does great things. "The LORD has done great things for us, Whereof we are glad" (Ps. 126:3).

"How precious also are Your thoughts to me, O God! How great is the sum of them" (Ps. 139:17).

God is thinking of you. His word speaks powerfully regarding this. The word of God tells us He loves us. The word of God tells us He cares about us. The word of God declares we should call upon Him and He will show us great and mighty things we do not know. All of these and numerous other scriptures add up to one gigantic fact: God is thinking of us.

The word of God is His thoughts to us. The totality of them is great in every sense.

When you come in the presence of God, remember you are in the atmosphere of greatness.

2. In His presence is honor and majesty.

"Honor and majestic are before Him…" (1 Chr 16:27)

Our God is honorable. He is to be honored above everyone else.

The word majesty means grandeur, dignity, nobility, splendor, distinction, eminence. The word majesty by its meaning greatly throws a mighty light regarding the nature of the presence of God. In His presence is unmatched distinction and splendor.

3. In His presence is Glory and Strength.

Strength and glory are in His place (1 Chr. 16:27). Where God is, you can definitely find strength and glory. Wherever you invite the presence of the Lord, you can find His strength and glory.

Strength means "resident power" so when you speak about the strength of the Lord, you are literally talking about the extent of the power of God. That, my dear friends is definitely unlimited.

The Psalmist believed in the strength of the Lord.

Ps. 18:1, "I will love You, O LORD, my strength."

Ps. 27:1, "The LORD is my light and my salvation; Whom shall I fear? The LORD is the strength of my life; of whom shall I be afraid?"

Ps. 71:16, "I will go in the strength of the LORD GOD. I will make mention of Your righteousness, of Yours only."

Ps. 73:26, "My flesh and my heart fail; But God is the strength of my heart and my portion forever."

You cannot do without the strength of the Lord. The strength of the Lord is what the Christian needs in his daily walk. The Apostle Paul wrote, "Be strong in the Lord, and in the power of His might."

Glory is in His place means where God is honor, respect, and adoration exist. It does not only exist there, it totally thrives in His presence. Our God is the God of glory. The world needs to know that our God should be glorified, praised, adored and honored in every extent possible. He is wonderful. He is awesome. He is worthy of our praise and honor.

4. In His presence is excellence.

   "Sing to the LORD, for He has done excellent things. This is known in all the earth" (Is. 12:5).

   "This also comes from the Lord of hosts, Who is wonderful in counsel and excellent in guidance" (Is. 23:29).

   He is an excellent God and does excellent things. When you come into His presence, you will be in the company of excellence.

5. In His presence is faithfulness.

   The faithfulness of God is described as:

   a. Everlasting.

       Ps. 119:90, Your faithfulness endures to all generations. You established the earth, and it abides."

   b. Established.

       "For I have said, "Mercy shall be built up forever. Your faithfulness You shall establish in the very heavens" (Ps. 89:2).

   c. Unfailing.

       Ps. 89:33, "Nevertheless My loving kindness I will not utterly take from him, nor allow My faithfulness to fail."

   d. Infinite.

       Ps. 36:5, "Your mercy, O LORD, is in the heavens, and Your faithfulness reaches to the clouds."

   e. Great.

       Lam 3:23, "…Great is Your faithfulness."

f. Incomparable.

Ps. 89:8, "O LORD God of hosts, Who is mighty like You, O LORD? Your faithfulness also surrounds You."

The faithfulness of God is manifested in:

a. Counsels.

Is. 25:1, "O LORD, You are my God. I will exalt You, I will praise Your name. For you have done wonderful things, Your counsels of old are faithfulness and truth.

b. Covenant-keeping.

Deut. 7:9, "Therefore know that the LORD your God, He is God, the faithful God who keeps covenant and mercy for a thousand generations with those who love Him and keep His commandments."

c. Testimonies.

Ps. 119:138, "Your testimonies, which You have commanded, are righteous and very faithful."

d. Judgments.

Jer. 51:29, "And the land will tremble and sorrow; For every purpose of the LORD shall be performed against Babylon. To make the land of Babylon a desolation without inhabitant.

e. Promises.

1 Kin. 8:20, "So the LORD has fulfilled His word which He spoke; and I have filled the position of my father David, and sit on the throne of Israel as the LORD promised; and I have built a house for the name of the LORD God of Israel."

When you come into the presence of God, remember you are in the company of One who is faithful.

6. In His presence is fullness of God.

> "...In His presence is fullness of God" (Ps. 16:11). In the presence of God, you can experience joy at His highest. This could explain the reason for the many that lack joy, they probably do not take the time to get into the presence of God.

The Psalmist knew of the joy of the Lord. Ps. 43:4, "Then I will go to the altar of God, to God my exceeding joy and on the harp I will praise You, O God, my God."

The scripture Ps. 16:11, "...In Your presence is fullness of joy; At your right hand are pleasures forevermore" plays a gigantic role concerning the presence of the Lord and the anointing. It brings into sharp focus a clear distinction between the two. This scripture presents two aspects, the presence of the Lord and His right hand. The presence of the Lord has to do with getting into His presence where you find fullness of joy. On the other hand, the right hand of God has to do with His power which is the anointing.

At the right hand of God there are pleasures forevermore. I thought, what does the scripture mean when it states there are pleasures forevermore? First, I had to make some distinction between fullness of joy and pleasures forevermore. In my estimation, whereas fullness of joy is great, pleasures forevermore remain greater. The presence of God provides a great aspect, but His right hand offers something greater. Pleasures forevermore in this sense offers the notion that you can attain many things that produces not only fullness of joy, but aspects that offers great pleasure. At the right hand of God, there is healing. At the right hand of God, there is salvation. At the right hand of God, there are miracles. At the right hand of God, there is Jesus. At the right hand of God, there is the power of God. At the right hand of God, there is the anointing.

Let me state another revelation. The fullness of joy or the oil of joy comes out of the anointing. In one of the messianic prophecies by Isaiah, which spoke of the anointing that was to be on Jesus Christ, the oil of joy was mentioned. Is. 61:1-3, "The Spirit of the Lord GOD is upon Me, because the LORD has anointed Me, to preach good tidings to the poor; He has sent Me to heal the brokenhearted, to proclaim liberty to the captives and the opening of the prison to those who are bound. To proclaim the acceptable year of the LORD, and the day of vengeance of our God; to comfort all who mourn. To console those who mourn in Zion, to give them beauty for ashes, the oil of joy for mourning, the garment of praise for the spirit of heaviness; that they may be called trees of righteousness, the planting of the LORD that He may be glorified." The anointing produces joy as one of its byproducts. The presence of the Lord also gives us joy. The anointing however goes further and offers many other aspects.

In the presence of the Lord, you can taste a little bit of what the anointing has to offer, but at His right hand you can have more. Get into his presence and proceed into His anointing, where His power can overcome every obstacle and produce every possible miracle.

The anointing, which is the power of God, is so precious and the Psalmists showed extreme positive altitude towards it. Ps. 21:13, "Be exalted. O LORD, in Your own strength! We will sing aloud of Your mercy in the morning; For You have been my defense and refuge in the day of my trouble." Ps. 145:11, "They shall speak of the glory of Your kingdom; and talk of your power."

CHAPTER 4
The Gateway To The Anointing

To be qualified to have the anointing you must be born again. There is no other way around it. Being born again is therefore probably the greatest gateway to the anointing. The primary reason for this is because when one is born again, the "Anointed One," the Christ comes in the power of His Spirit and lives inside of Him.

1 Cor. 2:9, "But as it is written: Eye has not seen, nor ear heard, nor have entered into the heart of man the things which God has prepared for those that love Him. But God has revealed them to us through His Spirit. For the Spirit searches all things, yes, the deep things of God."

From this verse of the scriptures, one fact comes out with extreme lucidity. It is the fact that the things of God cannot be realized, received or perceived by man unless they have the Spirit of God. This pertains to the anointing. The anointing cannot be perceived by man when He is not born again. If man cannot perceive the anointing, when He is not a child of God, then He definitely cannot be in possession of it.

Repeating the first gateway to the anointing stated above, you must be born again to qualify to have the anointing.

Isaiah 59:1, "Behold, the LORD's hand is not shortened, that it cannot save, nor His ear heavy that it cannot hear. But your iniquities have separated you from your God." Sin is what separates us from God. If one is not born again, they are living in sin and therefore separated from God. If such is the case with the individual then they definitely cannot have anything from God unless they repent and receive salvation. They therefore cannot receive the anointing unless they are born again and ask the Lord for it.

The Bible speaks of our condition before we were born again. Isaiah 1:4-6, "Alas, sinful nation, a people laden with iniquity, a brood of evildoers, children who are corruptors! They have forsaken the LORD. They have provoked to anger, the Holy One of Israel. They have turned backward. Why should you be stricken again? You will revolt more and more. The whole head is sick, and the whole heart faints. From the soil of the foot even to the head, there is no soundness in it. But wounds and bruises and putrefying sores, they have not been closed or bound up, or soothes with ointment."

Isaiah is like a miniature bible. The first thirty-nine chapters (like the thirty-nine books of the Old Testament) are filled with judgment upon immoral and idolatrous men. Judah has sinned; the surrounding nations have sinned, the whole earth has sinned. Judgment must come, for God cannot allow such blatant sin to go unpunished forever. But the final twenty-seven chapters (like the twenty-seven books of the New Testament) declare a message of hope. The Messiah is coming as a Savior and a Sovereign to bear a cross and to wear a crown (Open Bible, 675).

Isaiah 1:4-6, is found in the first part of Isaiah, and therefore holds the message of the sinful nature of Judah. This describes our condition before we were born again. The word of God declares the whole head is sick, this has definitely to do with the fact that, the head has not been able to perceive salvation offered by Jesus Christ. The whole head is sick because it contains ideas of ignorance and darkness, and not the word of God which produces light. The whole head is sick because it does not contain the message of God. The Bible declares that their whole heart faints because the God of all power has not been received. Their whole heart faints because they have not come to the realization that the One-true God can help them find themselves in any situation. They have not realized that God can be the strength of their heart. This realization has not been possible because they have not received Jesus Christ as Savior.

The word of God declares from the sole of the foot to the head, there is no soundness in it, but wounds and bruises and putrefying sores. They have not been closed or bound up, or soothes with ointment (Is. 1:6). The solution for such a person is a remedy from Almighty God. That remedy is the gospel of Jesus Christ. Receive Jesus Christ today.

An individual having such a condition who has not received the remedy God has offered, cannot receive the anointing.

The disciples of Christ also experience this first gateway to the anointing. "And when He had said this, He breathed on them, and said to them, Receive the Holy Spirit." Jesus breathing on the disciples and declaring for them to receive the Holy Spirit is equivalent to our salvation.

The second gateway to the anointing is simply to ask God for it.

"If you then, being evil, know how to give good gifts to your children, how much more will your Father who is in heaven give the Holy Spirit to those who ask Him" (Matt. 7:14). God gives the anointing when we ask Him for it.

The word of God declares, "Ask, and it will be given to you; seek, and you will find; knock, and it will be opened to you. For everyone who asks receives, and he who seeks finds, and to him who knocks it will be opened" (Matt 7:7-8).

When you ask, ask until you receive. God is willing to anoint you to do His work. Ask Him for His anointing.

The third gateway to the anointing is the element of faith. Faith unlocks miracles. Faith is an aspect that does not fail. It is a mighty element that is very important in Christianity.

The Apostle Paul writing to the Galatians wrote to them that the Holy Spirit is given by faith, not by works. Gal. 3:1-5, "O foolish Galatians! Who has bewitched you that you should not obey the truth, before whose eyes Jesus Christ was clearly portrayed among you as crucified? This only I want to learn from you. Did you receive the Spirit by the works of the law, or by the hearing of faith? Are you so foolish, having begun in the Spirit, are you now being made perfect by the flesh? Have you suffered so many things in vain—if indeed it was in vain? Therefore He who supplies the Spirit to you and works miracles among you, does He do it by the works of the law, or by the hearing of faith?

Through faith we receive the Holy Spirit. Through faith we receive the anointing.

Faith is an important element in the body of Christ. It is therefore worth looking into. Let us take the opportunity to divulge into this very essential aspect.

In defining faith Heb. 11:1, "Now faith is the substance of things hoped for, the evidence of things not seen." It can also be defined as confidence in the testimony of another. Relating it to the subject at hand, when we express our faith in the anointing, we are exhibiting our confidence in God's testimony regarding it.

The following factors are regarding the nature of faith:

   a.   Fruit of the Spirit.

        Gal. 5:22-23, "But the fruit of the Spirit is love, joy, peace, longsuffering, kindness, goodness, faithfulness, gentleness, self-control. Against such there is no law."

b. Work of God.

John 6:29, "Jesus answered and said to them, "This is the work of God, that you believe in Him whom He sent."

c. God's gift.

Eph. 2:8, "For by grace you have been saved through faith, and that not of yourselves, it is the gift of God."

d. Comes from the heart.

Rom. 10:9, 10, "That if you confess with your mouth the Lord Jesus and believe in your heart that God has raised Him from the dead, you will be saved. For with the heart one believes to righteousness, and with the mouth confession is made to salvation."

e. Substance of unseen things.

Heb. 11:1, "Now faith is the substance of things hoped for, the evidence of things not seen."

Faith results from the following:

a. Scriptures.

John 20:30-31, "And truly Jesus did many other signs in the presence of His disciples, which are not written in this book, but these are written that you may believe that Jesus is the Christ, the Son of God, and that believing you may have life in His name.

b. Preaching.

John 17:20, "I do not pray for these alone, but also for those who will believe in Me through their word.

c. Gospel.

Acts 15:7, "And when there had been much dispute, Peter rose up and said to them, 'Men and brethren, you know that a good while ago God chose among us, that by my mouth the Gentiles should hear the word of the gospel and believe.'"

The following are objects of faith.

a. God.

John 14:1, "Let not your heart be troubled, you believe in God, believe also in Me."

b. Christ.

John 20:31, "But these are written that you may believe that Jesus is the Christ, the Son of God, and that believing you may have life in His name."

c. Moses' writings.

John 5:46, "For if you believed Moses, you would believe Me, for he wrote about Me."

d. Writings of the prophets.

Acts 26:27, "King Agrippa, do you believe the prophets?"

e. Gospel.

Mark 1:15, "the time is fulfilled, and the kingdom of God is at hand, Repent, and believe in the gospel."

f. God's promises.

Rom. 4:21, "And being fully convinced that what He had promised He was also able to perform."

The following are the kinds of faith.

    a.   Saving.

            Rom 10:9-10, "That if you confess with your mouth, the Lord Jesus and believe in your heart that God has raised Him from the dead, you will be saved. For with the heart one believes unto righteousness, and with the mouth confession is made unto salvation."

    b.   Temporary.

            Luke 8:13, "But the ones on the rock are those who, when they hear, receive the word with joy, and these have no root, who believe for a while and in time of temptation fall away."

    c.   Intellectual.

            James 2:19, "You believe that there is one God. You do well. Even the demons believe and tremble."

    d.   Dead.

            James 2:17, 20, "Thus also faith by itself, if it does not have works, is dead," vs. 20, "But do you want to know, O foolish man, that faith without works is dead?"

Faith is described as:

    a.   Boundless.

            John 11:21-27, "Now Martha, said to Jesus, 'Lord if You have been here, my brother would not have died. But even now I know that whatever You ask of God, God will give You.' Jesus said to her, 'Your brother will rise again.' Martha said to Him, 'I know he will rise again in the resurrection at the last day.' Jesus said to her, 'I am the resurrection and the life. He who believes in Me, though he may die, he shall live. And whoever lives and believes in Me shall never die. Do you believe this?' She said to Him, 'Yes, Lord, I believe that You are the Christ, the Son of God, who is to come into the world.'"

b. Common.

Titus 1:4, "To Titus, my true son in our common faith. Grace, mercy and peace from God the Father and the Lord Jesus Christ our Savior."

c. Great.

Matt. 8:10, "Assuredly, I say to you, I have not found such great faith, not even in Israel!"

d. Holy.

Jude 20, "But you, beloved, building yourselves upon your most holy faith, praying in the Holy Spirit."

e. Humble.

Luke 7:6-7, "Then Jesus went with them. And when He was already not far from the house, the centurion sent friends to Him, saying to Him, "Lord, do not trouble Yourself, for I am not worthy that You should enter under my roof. Therefore I did not even think myself worthy to come to You. But say the word, and my servant will be healed."

f. Little.

Matt. 8:26, "But He said to them, 'Why are you fearful, O you of little faith?' Then He arose and rebuked the winds and the sea, and there was a great calm."

g.   Mutual.

Rom. 1:12, "That is, that I may be encouraged together with you by the mutual faith both of you and me."

h.   Perfect.

James 2:22, "Do you see that faith was working together with his works, and by works faith was made perfect?"

i.   Precious.

Luke 8:13, "But the ones on the rock are those who, when they hear, receive the word with joy, and these have no root, who believe for a while and in time of temptation fall away."

j.   Rootless.

Luke 8:13, "But the ones on the rock are those who, when they hear, receive the word with joy, and these have no root, who believe for a while and in time of temptation fall away."

k.   Small.

Matt. 17:20, "So Jesus said to them, 'Because of your unbelief, for assuredly, I say to you, if you have faith as a mustard seed, you will say to this mountain, 'Move from here to there,' and it will move; and nothing will be impossible for you.'"

l.   Unfeigned.

1 Tim. 1:5, "Now the end of the commandment is charity out of a pure heart, and of a good conscience, and of faith unfeigned."

m.   United.

Mark 2:5, "When Jesus saw their faith, He said to the paralytic, 'Son, your sins are forgiven you.'"

n.   Vain.

1 Cor. 15:14, 17, "And if Christ is not risen, then our preaching is empty and your faith is also empty" vs. 17, "And if Christ is not risen, your faith is futile, you are still in your sins!"

o.   Venturing.

Matt. 14:28, 29, "And Peter answered Him and said, 'Lord, if it is You, command me to come to You on the water.' So He said, 'Come.' And when Peter had come down out of the boat, he walked on the water to go to Jesus."

The fruits of faith are:

a.   Remission of sins.

Acts 10:43, "To Him all the prophets witness that, through His name, whoever believes in Him will receive remission of sins."

b.   Justification.

Acts 13:39, "And by Him everyone who believes is justified from all things from which you could not be justified by the law of Moses."

c.   Freedom from condemnation.

John 3:18, "He who believes in Him is not condemned, but he who does not believe is condemned, already, because he has not believed in the name of the only begotten Son of God."

d.   Salvation.

Mark 16:16, "He who believes and is baptized will be saved, but he who does not believe will be condemned."

e.   Sanctification.

Acts 15:9, "And made no distinction between us and them, purifying their hearts by faith."

f.   Freedom from spiritual death.

John 11:25-26, "Jesus said to her, 'I am the resurrection and the life. He who believes in Me, though he may die, he shall live. And whosoever lives and believes in Me shall never die. Do you believe this?'"

g.   Spiritual light.

John 12:36, 46, "While you have the light, believe in the light, that you may become 'sons of light.'"

h.   Spiritual life.

John 20:31, "But these are written that you may believe that Jesus is the Christ, the Son of God, and that believing you may have life in His name."

i.   Eternal life.

John 3:15-16, "For God so loved the world that He gave His only begotten Son, that whoever believes in Him should not perish but have everlasting life. For God did not send His Son into the world to condemn the world, but that the world through Him might be saved.

j.   Adoption.

John 1:12, "But as many as received Him, to them He gave the right to become the children of God, to those who believe in His name."

k.   Access to God.

Eph. 3:12, "In whom we have boldness and access with confidence through faith in Him."

l.   Edification.

1 Tim. 1:4, "Neither give heed to fables and endless genealogies, which minister questions, rather than godly edifying which is in faith; so do."

m.   Preservation.

John 10:26-29, "But you do not believe because you are not of My sheep, as I said to you. My sheep hear My voice, and I know them, and they follow Me. And I give them eternal life, and they shall never perish; neither shall anyone snatch them out of My hand."

n.   Inheritance.

Acts 26:18, "To open their eyes, in order to turn them from darkness to light, and from the power of Satan to God, that they may receive forgiveness of sins, and an inheritance among those who are sanctified by faith in Me."

o.   Peace and rest.

Rom. 5:1, "Therefore having been justified by faith, we have peace with God through our Lord Jesus Christ."

The following are the places of faith in the Christian life:

a. Live by.

Rom. 1:17, "For in it the righteousness of God is revealed from faith to faith, as it is written, 'The just shall live by faith.'"

b. Walk by.

Rom. 4:12, "And the father of circumcision to those who not only are of the circumcision, but who also walk in the steps of the faith which our father Abraham had while still uncircumcised."

c. Pray by.

Matt. 21:22, "And whatever things you ask in prayer, believing, you will receive."

d. Resist evil by.

Eph. 6:16, "Above all, taking the shield of faith with which you will be able to quench all the fiery darts of the wicked one."

e. Overcome world by.

1 John 2:13-17, "I write to you, little children because your sins are forgiven you for His name's sake. I write to you, Fathers, because you have known Him who is from the beginning. I write to you, young men, because you have overcome the wicked one, I write to you, young men, because you have overcome the wicked on, I write to you, little children, because you have known the Father. I have written to you, Fathers, because you have known Him who is from the beginning. I have written to you, young men, because you are strong and the word of God abides in you, and you have overcome the

wicked one. Do not love the world of the things in the world. If anyone loves the world, the love of the Father is not in him. For all that is in the world, the lust of the flesh, the lust of the eyes, is of the world. and the world is passing away, and the lust of it, but he who does the will of God abides forever."

f.   Die in.

Heb. 11:13, "These all died in faith, not having received the promises, but having seen them afar off were assured of them, embraced them, and confessed that they were strangers and pilgrims on the earth.

The growth of faith, in the Christian life is as follows:

a.   Stand fast in.

1 Cor. 16:13, "Watch, stand fast in the faith, be brave, be strong.

b.   Continue in.

Acts 14:22, "Strengthening the souls of the disciples, exhorting them to continue in the faith, and saying, "We must through many tribulations enter the Kingdom of God."

c.   Be strong in.

Rom 4:20-24, "He did not waver at the promise of God through unbelief, but was strengthened in faith, giving glory to God, and being fully convinced that what He had promised, He was also able to perform. And therefore, 'it was accounted to him for righteousness.' Now it was not written for his sake alone that it was imputed to him, but also for us. It shall be imputed to use who believe in Him who raised up Jesus our Lord from the dead."

d.   Abound in.

2 Cor. 8:7, "But as you abound in everything, in faith, in speech, in knowledge, in all diligence, and in your love for us, see that you abound in this grace also."

e.   Be grounded in.

Col. 1:23, "If indeed you continue in the faith, rounded and steadfast, and are not moved away from the hope of the gospel which you heard, which was preached to every creature under heaven, of which, 1 Paul became a minister."

f.   Hold fast.

1 Tim 1:19, "Holding faith, and a good conscience, which some having put away concerning faith have made shipwreck."

g.   Pray for increase of.

Luke 17:5, "And the apostles said to the Lord, 'Increase our faith.'"

h.   Have assurance of 2 Tim 1:12, "For that which cause I also suffer these things nevertheless I am not ashamed for I know whom I have believed, and am persuaded that he is able to keep that which I have committed unto him against that day."

As we had established earlier, faith remains paramount in our seeking for the anointing. As Christians, let us stand fast in faith. Continue in faith. Stay strong in faith. Abound in faith. Stay grounded in faith. Hold fast to faith. Pray for the increase of faith. Have assurance of faith.

We can reach God with this ever important aspect called faith, and release the anointing.

CHAPTER 5
Proven Anointing

The Bible declares that the word of God is proven (Ps. 18:30). The word prove means to demonstrate, test or establish the validity. The anointing, which is part of the word of God, has been demonstrated through generations to be true. It is mightily time tested to be true. It has been enormously established through time to be of an outstanding validity. The anointing is true. The anointing is proven.

Thinking about the proven nature of the anointing, it is worthwhile to comment on certain facts that play a gigantic role in that regard.

Let us look at Luke 4:17-21, "And He was handed the book of the prophet Isaiah. And when He had opened the book, He found the place where it was written: The Spirit of the LORD is upon Me, Because He has anointed Met to preach the gospel to the poor. He has sent Me to heal the broken hearted. To preach deliverance to the captives, and recovery of sight to the blind, to set at liberty those who are oppressed. to preach the acceptable year of the LORD. then He closed the book, and gave it back to the attendant and sat down. And the eyes of all who were in the synagogue were fixed on Him. And He began to say to them, "Today this Scripture is fulfilled in your hearing."

When Jesus spoke the statement, "Today, this Scripture is fulfilled in your hearing," it speaks volumes to the fact that the anointing from that very instant was destined to be proven. Jesus went from there and demonstrated the power of God.

Let us discuss a few of the miracles of Jesus to announce the fact that the anointing is proven.

"On the third day there was a wedding in Cana of Galilee, and the mother of Jesus was there. Now both Jesus and His disciples were invited to the wedding. And when they ran out of wine, the mother of Jesus said to Him, 'They have no wine.' Jesus said to her, 'Woman, what does your concern have to do with Me? My hour has not yet come.' His mother said to the servants, 'Whatever He says to you, do it.' Now there were set there six water pots of stone, according to the manner of purification of the Jews, containing twenty or thirty gallons apiece. Jesus said to them, 'Fill the water pots with water.' And they filled them to the brim. And He said to them, 'Draw some out now, and take it to the master of the feast.' And they took it. When the master of the feast had tasted the water that was made wine, and did not know where it came from (but the servants who had drawn the water knew), the master of the feast called the bridegroom. And he said to him, 'Every man at the beginnings sets out the good wine, and when the guests have all drunk, then the inferior. You have kept the good wine until now!' This beginning of signs Jesus did in Cana of Galilee, and manifested His glory, and His disciples believed in Him" (John 2:1-11).

In the above, John records the first miracle Jesus performed. Here we see the anointing was proven. Water was turned into wine. His disciples believed in Him.

"When Jesus heard it, He departed from there by boat to a deserted place by Himself. But when the multitude heard it, they followed Him on foot from the cities. And when

Jesus went out He saw a great multitude; and He was moved with compassion for them and healed their sick. When it was evening, His disciples came to Him, saying 'this is a deserted place and the hour is already late. Send the multitudes away, that they may go into the villages and buy themselves food.' But Jesus said to them, 'They do not need to go away. You give them something to eat.' And they said to Him, 'We have here only five loaves and two fish.' He said, 'Bring them here to Me.' Then He commanded the multitudes to sit down on the grass. And he took the five loaves and the two fish, and looking up to heaven, He blessed and broke and gave the loaves to the disciples, and the disciples gave to the multitudes. So they all ate and were filled, and they took up twelve baskets full of the fragments that remained. Now those who had eaten were about five thousand men, besides women and children" (Matt. 14:13-21). Here again, the anointing is proven. The feeding of the five thousand is a mighty miracle and ushers in the concept that the anointing has no impossibilities, just possibilities.

Jesus performed many healings. When you read the gospels, one fact comes out with every lucidity, and it is that He is a healing Jesus. His healings show that the anointing is proven.

"Then His fame went throughout all Syria, and they brought to Him all sick people who were afflicted with various diseases and torments, and those who were demon-possessed, epileptics, and paralytics, and He healed them" (Matt. 4:24).

"When he had come down from the mountain, great multitudes followed Him. And behold, a leper came and worshiped Him, saying, 'Lord, if You are willing, You can make me clean.' Then Jesus put out His hand and touched him, saying, 'I am willing, be cleansed.' Immediately his leprosy was cleansed" (Matt. 8:1-4).

"Now when Jesus had come into Peter's house, He saw his wife's mother lying sick with a fever. So He touched her hand, and the fever left her. And she arose and served them. When evening had come, they brought to Him many who were demon-possessed. And He cast out the spirits with a word, and healed all who were sick, that it might be fulfilled which was spoken by Isaiah the prophet, saying: 'He Himself took our infirmities, and bore our sickness'" (Matt 18:14-17).

"But when Jesus knew it, He withdraws from there. and great multitudes followed Him, and He healed them all" (Matt. 12:15).

"Then one was brought to Him who was demon-possessed, blind and mute, and He healed him, so that the blind and mute man both spoke and saw" (Matt. 12:22).

"Then great multitudes came to Him, having with them the lame, blind, mute, maimed, and many others; and they laid them down at Jesus' feet, and He healed them" (Matt. 15:30).

"And great multitudes followed Him, and He healed them there" (Matt.19:2).

"Then He healed many who were sick with various diseases, and cast out many demons; and He did not allow the demons to speak, because they knew Him" (Mark 1:34).

"For He healed many, so that as many as had afflictions pressed about Him to touch Him" (Mark 3:10).

"Now a certain woman had a flow of blood for twelve years, and had suffered many things from many physicians. She had spent all that she had and was no better, but rather grew worse. When she heard about Jesus, she came behind Him in the crowd and touched His garment. For she said, 'If only I may touch His clothes, I shall be made well.' Immediately the fountain of her blood was dried up, and she felt in her body that she was healed of the affliction" (Mark 5:25-29).

"When the sun was setting, all those who had any that were sick with various diseases brought them to Him; and He laid His hands on every one of them and healed them" (Luke 4:40).

"And He came down with them and stood on a level place with a crowd of His disciples and a great multitude of people from all Judea and Jerusalem, and from the seacoast of Tyre and

Sidon, who came to hear Him and be healed of their diseases, as well as those who were tormented with unclean spirits. And they were healed. And the whole multitude sought to touch Him, for power went out from Him and healed them all" (Luke 6:17-19).

"But when the multitudes knew it, they followed Him; and He received them and spoke to them about the Kingdom of God, and healed those who had need of healing" (Luke 9:11).

"And as he was still coming, the demon threw him down and convulsed him. Then Jesus rebuked the unclean spirit, healed the child, and gave him back to the father" (Luke 9:42).

"But they kept silent. And He took him and healed him, and let him go" (Luke 14:4).

The proven nature of the anointing can be thought of in terms of Mark 16:17-18 which states, "And these signs will follow those who believe: In My name they will cast out demons; they will speak with new tongues; they will take up serpents; and if they drink anything deadly, it will by no means hurt them; they will lay hands on the sick and they will recover." In other words, Jesus is saying, if we believe in His name, we will operate under the anointing, and see proven results.

Another aspect that speaks of the proven nature of the anointing in my estimation is Hebrews 13:8 which reads, "Jesus is the same yesterday, today and forever."

God is still performing miracles. The anointed are still seeing proven results. The miracles of God are still seen by men and women anointed of God.

Another aspect worthy of notation is that since the Lord's anointing is proven, ours is as well. "Most assuredly, I say to you, he who believes in Me, the works that I do he will do also, and greater works than these he will do, because I go to my Father" (John 14:12). In other words, Jesus is saying the miracles you see me perform, you can do the same and even greater if you believe in Him.

His anointing is proven, therefore ours will do the same. Our anointing comes from Him.

This chapter was written for an enormous reason. It is to bring into sharp focus the ability of the anointing, and to announce that it is extremely productive. The ability of the anointing is unlimited. You can depend upon its influence to see darling results.

Get anointed. Let God use you to touch this world for Him bringing out every proven outcome.

CHAPTER 6
The Goodness Of The Lord And The Anointing

In writing this book, I was directed by the Spirit about the connection that exists between the anointing and the goodness of God. I think it is an aspect worth looking into.

Let us take the opportunity to explore the word of God regarding His goodness. "I will make all my goodness pass before you; and I will proclaim the name of the LORD before you" (Ex. 33:19). "And it shall be, if you go with us, indeed it shall be that whatever good the LOD will do to us, the same we will do to you" (Num. 10:32).

"And now, O Lord God, you are God, and Your words are true, and You have promised this goodness to Your servant" (2 Sam 7:28).

"On the eighth day he sent the people away; and they blessed the king, and went in their tents joyful and glad of heart for all the good that the LORD had done for His servant David, and for Israel, His people" (1 Kings 8:66).

"And now, LORD, You are God, and have promised this goodness to Your servant" (1 Chr. 17:26).

"Now therefore, Arise, O LORD God, to Your resting place, You and the ark of Your strength. Let Your priests, O LORD God, be clothed with salvation, and let Your saints rejoice in goodness" (2 Chr. 6:41).

"And they took strong cities and a rich land, and possessed houses full of all goods, cisterns already dug, vineyards, olive groves, and fruit trees in abundance. So they ate and were filled and grew fat. And delighted themselves in Your goodness" (Neh. 9:25).

"For You meet him with the blessings of goodness. You set a crown of pure gold upon his head" (Ps. 21:3).

"Do not remember the sins of my youth, nor my transgressions. According to Your mercy, remember me. For Your goodness sake, O LORD" (Ps. 25:7).

"He loves righteousness and justice. The earth is full of the goodness of the LORD" (Ps. 33:5).

"You crown the year with Your goodness, and Your paths drip with abundance" (Ps. 65:11).

"Oh, that men would give thanks to the LORD for His goodness, and for His wonderful works to the children of men. For He satisfies the longing soul, and fills the hungry soul with goodness" (Ps. 107:8-9).

"I will mention the loving kindness of the LORD, and the praises of the LORD, according to all that the LORD has bestowed on us, and the great goodness toward the house of Israel, which He has bestowed on them according to His mercies, according to the multitude of His loving kindness" (Is. 63:7).

"Then it shall be to Me a name of joy, a praise, and an honor before all nations of the earth, who shall hear all the good that I do to them; they shall fear and tremble for all the goodness and all the prosperity that I provide for it" (Jer. 33:9).

"Afterward the children of Israel shall return and seek the LORD their God and David their King. They shall fear the LORD and His goodness in the latter days" (Hos. 3:5).

"Or do you despise the riches of His goodness, forbearance, and longsuffering, not knowing that the goodness of God leads you to repentance?" (Rom. 2:4).

"But the fruit of the Spirit is love, joy, peace, longsuffering, kindness, goodness, faithfulness" (Gal. 5:22).

"For the fruit of the Spirit is in all goodness, righteousness, and truth" (Eph. 5:9).

"Therefore we also pray always for you that our God would count you worthy of this calling, and fulfill all the good pleasure of His goodness and the work of faith with power" (2 Thess. 1:11).

The goodness of God is one of God's essential attributes. It is described as:

    a.   Abundant.

          Ex. 34:6, "And the LORD passed before him and proclaimed, 'The LORD, the LORD God, merciful and gracious, longsuffering, and bounding in goodness and truth.'"

          In describing, the goodness of God as abundant, there is ample documentation to prove the fact as being true to every degree. God has reached mankind with goodness in virtually every area of his life. This endeavor is still in process. God's nature of goodness is an aspect that is constantly being offered and planted in our lives. It comes in numerous shapes and sizes and offers us benefits that is unmatched in any sphere. Individual examination is required to expose this abundant goodness of God. Try it and you will end up ever thankful to our great God.

b.   Great.

"Oh, how great is Your goodness, which You have laid up for those who fear You, which You have prepared for those who trust in You, in the presence of the sons of men" (Ps. 31:19).

God is a great God, and His deeds can be described in terms of that as well. His goodness is great because He loves you, He wants what is best for you. His goodness offered to you is wrapped up in greatness, so that is influence will be a maximum in your life. This great goodness is extended to those that fear and trust in God.

c.   Enduring.

"Why do you boast in evil, O magnify man? The goodness of God endures continually" (Ps. 52:1).

God's goodness is a continual aspect to you because of His love. God's love for you is everlasting and its byproduct, His goodness, also remains enduring.

d.   Satisfying.

Blessed is the man You choose, and cause to approach You, that he may dwell in Your courts. We shall be satisfied with the goodness of Your house, of Your holy temple" (Ps. 65:4).

e.   Universal.

"The Lord is good to all, and His tender mercies are over all His works" (Ps. 145:9).

The goodness of God is manifested in the following.

a.   Material blessings.

"That you may be sons of Your Father in heaven; for He makes His sun rise on the evil and on the good, and sends rain on the just and on the unjust" (Matt. 5:45). "Nevertheless, He did not leave Himself without witness, in that He did good, gave us rain from heaven and fruitful seasons, filling our hearts with food and gladness" (Acts 14:17)

b.   Spiritual blessings.
Ps. 31:19, "Oh, how great is Your goodness, which You have laid up for those who trust in You, in the presence of the sons of men."

c.   Forgiving sin.
Ps. 86:5, "For, You, Lord, are good, and ready to forgive, and abundant in mercy to all those who call upon You."

The saints attitude toward the goodness of God are the following:

a.   Rejoice.
Ex. 18:9, "Then Jethro rejoiced for all the good which the LORD had done for Israel, whom He had delivered out of the hand of the Egyptians."

b.   Remember.
Ps. 145:7, "They shall utter the memory of Your great goodness, and shall sing of Your righteousness."

c.   Be satisfied with.
Jer. 31:14, "I will satiate the soul of the priests with abundance, and My people shall be satisfied with My goodness, says the LORD."

The Bible declares that the goodness of God leads to repentance (Romans 2:4).

The fact becomes clear, which is that it was God's goodness that caused Him to send His Son to die for the sins of mankind.

If one accepts the redemptive work done by Christ, they become a new creation, the righteousness of God in Jesus Christ, thereby being viable to receive the Spirit of God and the anointing. It is therefore safe to declare that if it was not for the goodness of God, the anointing will not be available to us. It can further be stated the goodness of God leads to repentance and then to the anointing.

The goodness of God compels Him to have a wonderful plan for mankind. He does not want anyone to perish, but to have everlasting life. He wants all to spend eternity with Him. 2 Peter 3:9 reads, "The Lord is not slack concerning His promise, as some count slackness, but is longsuffering toward us, not willing that any should perish but that all should come to repentance."

The goodness of God causes Him to think admirably toward us.

For I know the thoughts that I think toward you, says the LORD, thoughts of peace and not of evil, to give you a future and a hope" (Jer. 29:11).

"Beloved, I pray that you may prosper in all things, and be in health, just as your soul prospers" (3 John 2).

The goodness of God causes Him to intend good for us in every area of our lives. His goodness also causes Him to act admirably toward us.

Thinking about God's goodness and the anointing, we can make some bold statements, which in my estimation really are relevant.

God has anointed us because He is good. His anointing upon our lives is purely related to the fact that He acted upon His goodness. God's goodness paved the way for His anointing to become part of our lives.

God has anointed us that we remain a channel of His goodness. "How God anointed Jesus of Nazareth with the Holy Spirit and with power, who went about doing good and healing all who were oppressed by the devil, for God was with

Him" (Acts 10:38). When we get anointed, we are bound to exhibit the goodness of God. The power of God opens our heart, fills it with His love, enabling His goodness to flow out of it. It is extremely worthwhile to pray that God will use us as instruments of His goodness.

The goodness of God is an essential element and its benefits to us are extremely important in helping us grasp knowledge of His dealings, furthermore in aiding us in getting acquainted with Him.

Thank you God for your goodness and for your anointing.

CHAPTER 7

Purposes Of The Anointing

1.   The anointing destroys the yoke.

      "It shall come to pass in that day, that his burden will be taken away from your shoulder, and his yoke from your neck, and the yoke will be destroyed because of the anointing oil" (Isaiah 10:27).

2.   The anointing teaches you all things.

      "But the anointing which you have received from Him abides in you, and you do not need that anyone teach you; but as the same anointing teaches you concerning all things, and is true, and is not a lie, and just as it has taught you, you will abide in Him" (1 John 2:27).

3.   The anointing consecrates you and sets you apart to do something specific.

4.   You are weak in places so the anointing fills in those cracks to allow you to do what God calls you to do; it makes you strong.

5.   It is your saving strength.

6.   It is the oil of joy, the joy of the Lord is your strength.

7.   The anointing is both vertical, coming down from God to you in personal relationships, and horizontal, going out to touch others.

8.   It equips you with the miracle power of God to do the works of Jesus. You can do greater works than Jesus did.

9.   It makes you a dynamic soul winner.

10.   In Luke 4:18, Jesus declared the purpose of the anointing, and it is extremely conclusive in its nature. Here, He outlined six different aspects which completely denotes the purpose of the anointing.

    a.   To preach the gospel to the poor.
    b.   To heal the broken hearted.
    c.   To preach deliverance to the captives.
    d.   Recovery of sight to the blind.
    e.   To set at liberty those who are bruised.
    f.   To preach the acceptable year of the Lord.

The anointing was extremely great in the life of Jesus Christ. In His ministry He walked in the purpose of the anointing and did great deeds to glorify God. The woman with the issue of blood was healed instantly when she touched the hem of Jesus' garment. The anointing on Jesus saturated the clothes He wore. The power in the life of Jesus was to help people. It was to help humanity in any need. His power is so mighty. It can heal, deliver and set you free. Jesus' hands transferred the anointing to heal people. Jesus spoke Words of Spirit and life and people were made whole.

Peter's shadow fell on people and they were healed. That definitely showed that the anointing of God is extremely powerful. It also divulges the heart of God, which is that He wants His power to touch and heal humanity, to the extent that the shadow of a man brought healing. God is wonderful. He is ever helpful. He wants you well. He has designed His anointing to reach mankind with the greatest good.

Cloths and aprons taken from Paul's body were placed on the sick and they recovered and were delivered. His anointing works.

When a dead man was buried on top of Elijah's bones, he revived because of the anointing upon Elijah. The anointing is powerful. The purpose of the anointing is to help in any situation. All things are possible with the anointing.

The anointing comes from God, and there is nothing impossible with God, therefore the anointing can bring about every possibility.

As a Christian, you need to believe what God says about you, and move in the anointing and let its purposes be spread in this world. As a believer, you are the righteousness of God, you are a new creation, you are a partaker of the divine nature, you are full of the Holy Spirit, you are the anointed of God, the greater One lives in you, you are a king and priest, you are forgiven, cleansed, saved, and redeemed by the blood of Jesus, you are bold as a lion, you are without condemnation, you are free from fear, weakness and inferiority, you are living in divine health, you are led by the Holy Spirit, and you are walking in the wisdom of God. Above all, you have God on your side, let His anointing flow through you and touch this world, so that His purpose can be printed boldly everywhere. God is counting on you. Get anointed.

CHAPTER 8

Touch The World

There is a classic formula designed by God to be used in touching this world for Him, and it is found in Zechariah 4:6, "Not by might, nor by power, but by My Spirit." Here, God declares that it will not take human ability to do His work, it will take His Spirit. It was the Spirit of God that enabled Peter and John to touch their world for Jesus Christ. "Now when they saw the boldness of Peter and John, and perceived that they were uneducated and untrained men, they marveled. And they realized that they had been with Jesus" (Acts 4:13).

The Sanhedrin consisted of leading priests and elders who were permitted by the Roman government to have jurisdiction over religious and civic matters. Annas was a former high priest and Caiaphas was the present one. These people including members of the family of the High Priest and others, were marveled concerning the anointing on Peter and John. The fact that Peter and John had no technical religious training, and could be so bold, and mightily used by God, marveled them. However, they reached a very delicious conclusion: THEY

REALIZED THAT THEY HAD BEEN WITH JESUS. The anointing on the life of Peter and John was the result of the Holy Spirit who came to them in fulfillment of Jesus' promise (John 15:26,27). Our own personal relationship with God and His Spirit should be so evident as to cause those who hear us to conclude that we have been with Jesus.

It must be realized that being with Jesus is an enormous venture, it will give you the anointing to transform and touch your world for God.

What does it mean to be with Jesus? It means to spend time with Him in prayer. We must pray and seek His face every day. We must pray, so that He can empower us to touch the world, for His glory. The Apostles' prayed for boldness and the anointing. "Now, Lord, look on their threats, and grant to Your servants that with all boldness they may speak Your word, by stretching out Your hand to heal, and that signs and wonders may be done through the name of Your holy Servant Jesus Christ" (Acts 4:29-30).

In the very next verse, we read that God answered their prayer, "And when they had prayed, the place where they were assembled together was shaken; and they were all filled with the Holy Spirit, and they spoke the word of God with boldness" (Acts 4:31).

Prayer is paramount in our endeavor to touch the world for Jesus Christ. There is no other way, it is the only avenue through which we can be empowered to do His work.

The word of God declares, "The fervent prayer of a righteous man availeth much" (James 5:16). This verse of the scriptures, literally mans the continual praying of a righteous man makes tremendous power available. Therefore, if we are to receive great power we must continue to pray everyday. This power that we receive in prayer is the anointing, the major ingredient in touching this world for His glory.

God wants us to be anointed so that we can touch the world for His glory. "But you shall receive power when the Holy

Spirit has come upon you; and you shall be witnesses to me in Jerusalem, and in all Judea and Samaria, and to the end of the earth." Notice in this verse of the Scriptures, Jesus declared, "You shall be witnesses to Me." This indicates that our message is about Jesus. That is the only message the world needs to hear. The word of God is very clear concerning this fact.

"Nor is there salvation in any other, for there is no other name under heaven given among men by which we must be saved" (Acts 4:12).

The book of Acts contain several sermons. One of the most eloquent sermons in the Book of Acts is Paul's speech to the Athenian philosophers from the Areopagus, or Mars' Hill, a strong point named for the Greek god of war, Ares (Roman god, Mars). This hill overlooked the city of Athens. In his speech, Paul declared that God will hold all people accountable for their responses to His Son (Acts 17) (Open Bible, 1572).

The Book of Acts records sermons in the following verses:
Acts 12:14-40
Acts 3:12-26
Acts 4:5-12
Acts 7
Acts 10:28-47
Acts 11:4-18
Acts 13:16-41
Acts 15:7-11
Acts 15:13-21
Acts 20:17-35
Acts 22:1-21
Acts 23:1-6
Acts 26
Acts 28:17-20

The underlying message in all of these is Jesus. He is the One the world needs to know. He is the Savior of the world.

Thinking about the message of Jesus Christ, a portrait of Him can be seen in every book of the Bible. He is the central figure of Christianity. He is our everything. The entire word of God proclaims who He is in a mighty way.

In Genesis, He is the seed of the woman.

In Exodus, He is our Prophet, Priest, and King.

In Leviticus, He is our High Priest.

In Numbers, He is our rock.

In Deuteronomy, He is our savior and intercessor.

In Joshua, He is the captain of the host of the LORD.

In Judges, He is our Prophet, Priest, and King.

In Ruth, He is our kinsman-redeemer.

In 1 Samuel, He is our Prophet, Priest, and King.

In 2 Samuel, He is our King.

In 1 King, He became to us wisdom from God.

In 2 Kings, He emphasizes grace, life, and hope.

In 1 chronicles, He is our Prophet, Priest, and King.

In 2 Chronicles, He is the temple.

In Ezra, He forgives and restores.

In Nehemiah, He restores.

In Esther, He is our advocate.

In Job, He is our Life, Redeemer, Mediator and Advocate.

In Psalms, He is the "Anointed One."

In Proverbs, He is our wisdom.

In Ecclesiastes, He is our Shepherd.

In Song of Solomon, We will be the bride of Christ.

In Isaiah, He is our Savior, our Healer.

In Jeremiah, He is the coming Shepherd.

In Lamentations, He is the man of sorrows who was acquainted with grief.

In Ezekiel, He is the true Shepherd.

In Daniel, He is the Son of Man, and the coming Messiah.

In Hosea, He is our redeemer.

In Joel, He is the who will judge the nations.

In Amos, He is the judge, and He will also restore His people.

In Obadiah, He is the Judge of the nations, the Savior of Israel, and the possessor of the kingdom.

In Jonah, He shall be three days and three nights in the heart of the earth.

In Micah, He will be born in Bethlehem.

In Nahum, He is he Judge of the nations.

In Habakkuk, He is our Savoir.

In Zechariah, He is the Judge.

In Haggai, He is the One who gives peace.

In Zechariah, He is both Servant and King, Man and God.

In Malachi, He is the coming Lord.

In Matthew, He is "the son of Man," the "Servant" of the Lord.

In Mark, He is an active, compassionate, and obedient Servant.

In Luke, He is the Son of Man.

In John, He is the Son of God.

In Acts, He is the resurrected Savior.

In Romans, His death and resurrection are the basis for the believer's redemption, justification, reconciliation, salvation, and glorification.

In 1 Corinthians, He became to us wisdom from God.

In 2 Corinthians, He is our comfort, triumph, Lord, light, judge, reconciliation, substitute, gift, owner, and power.

In Galatians, He has delivered us from the curse of sin, law, and self.

In Ephesians, the believer is in Christ, in the heavenly places in Him, chosen in Him, adopted through Him.

In Philippians, He is our life, He is the source of our power over circumstances.

In Colossians, He is our life, the source of the believer's power for a new life.

In 1 and 2 Thessalonians, He is coming soon.

In 1 and 2 Timothy, He is the only mediator between God and man.

In Titus, He is our Redeemer.

In Philemon, He forgives.

In Hebrews, He is our eternal High Priest.

In James, He is Lord.

In 1 Peter, He is our example and Chief Shepherd.

In 2 Peter, He is Lord.

In 1 John, He is our righteous Advocate before the Father.

In 2 John, we must abide in the teaching of Christ to have a relationship with God.

In 3 John, Christ is the source and incarnation of truth.

In Jude, the believer is "kept for Christ."

In Revelation, He is the faithful witness, the first and the last, the living One, the Son of God, holy and true, the Lion of the tribe of Judah, the Word of God, King of Kings, and Lord of Lords, the Alpha and Omega, the bright and morning star, and the Lord Jesus Christ.

The Word of God is full of the message of Christ, and it is this that the world needs. When the Lord called me to preach, He spoke a phrase to me, and it is, "the Message is Christ." God was telling me that was the message the world needs to hear and I was to preach that. All the messages I have preached reflect that statement. The reason for God's anointing is for us to preach Jesus to this dying world.

Coming back to Acts 1:8, "God wants us to be witnesses of Jesus in Jerusalem, and in all Judea and Samaria, and even to the outermost parts of the earth."

God has provided His anointing that we can touch the world for His glory. God's anointing is for world evangelism. We must pray for God to use us in touching this world for Him.

Those with the anointing on their lives have the capability to be world-changers. The anointing is designed for a world-changing purpose. It is the greatest tool needed to touch this world.

We must strive to be greatly anointed for world evangelism. There is a price to pay for the anointing. We have to deny ourselves. We have to wait in the presence of God. We have to die to our plans and live for God's. It takes a consecrated lifestyle of daily Bible reading, regular prayer, and fasting.

"The young lions lack and suffer hunger, but those who seek the LORD shall not lack any good thing" (Ps. 34:10). The anointing is a good thing. It is precious, and a tremendous treasure. When you seek the Lord, God will make it available to you. The reason why many are not anointed may just be because they do not seek the Lord.

Children of God, rise up and seek the Lord, He will anoint you to touch this world for Him.

God has so much anointing. He is looking for men and women who will seek Him in regular fasting and praying so that He can let His mighty anointing fall on them.

The anointing is for touching this world because it produces miracles. Through the anointing people are saved, healed, delivered, and set free.

Thinking about touching this world for God, let us consider the Great Commission. "Go into all the world and preach the gospel to all creation" (Mark 16:15). In other words, Jesus is saying touch this world for me. His heart is for this world to know, who He is, and to be saved.

Looking again at the Great Commission, Mark 16:15, a number of factors can be deduced from it.

1. The Gospel must be preached.

Mark 16:15 speaks of the very heart of God and His desire for men to be saved. The gospel is the message of repentance and God wants us to preach so that men and women become aware of it, and turn from their sins and become His children.

2. Tell them of His love.

The gospel of Jesus Christ is about His love for mankind. When the gospel is shared, the world will become aware of God's love for them. In giving of the Great Commission, Jesus was desiring for the world to know His love for them. It was the love of God that brought about His redemptive work.

3. Tell them of My Benefits.

The gospel is God's ultimate goodness for mankind. The benefits of the gospel are listed in Psalm 103:1-5, "Bless, the LORD, O my soul; and all that is within me, bless His holy name. Bless the LORD, O my soul, and forget not His benefits. Who forgives all your iniquities, who heals all your diseases, who redeems your life from destruction, who crowns you with loving kindness and tender mercies, who satisfies your mouth with good things, so that your youth is renewed like the eagle's."

Here, you can see the psalmist exhorts himself to give praise to the Lord with his whole being. The benefits listed above are to do with redemption and renewal. That is what the gospel is about, and it is the heart of God that the world knows what is available to them.

The great message of the gospel can effectively be preached to touch this world by the anointing of the Holy Spirit.

Remember, you cannot touch this world by your personal ability, but by the Spirit of God. Get anointed. Let God use you for His glory.

I want to agree with the readers of this book for God's anointing upon their lives. If you've been seeking for the anointing to be mighty upon you, take this opportunity to pray with me.

"FATHER, THAT YOU FOR SENDING JESUS CHRIST TO DIE ON THE CROSS FOR MY SINS.

THANK YOU FOR MY SALVATION. FILL ME WITH THE HOLY SPIRIT AND ANOINT ME WITH POWER TO CHANGE THIS WORLD FOR YOUR GLORY IN JESUS N AME. AMEN.

I feel the anointing of the Holy Spirit as I write the above prayer. I believer God is about to do something special in your life. Write to me and let me know what God has done for you.

Write to:
Dr. George Moore
PO Box 4857
Panorama City, CA 91412
U.S.A.

ABOUT THE AUTHOR

Dr. George Moore is an international Evangelist. He has preached the gospel in Haiti, Dominican Republic, Jamaica, Puerto Rico, Brazil, Ghana, Nigeria, and the United States. His television program, "The Message is Christ" airs on Time Warner, Adelphia, and Comcast cable television stations in the East San Fernando Valley, West San Fernando Valley, and Tujunga areas of California, U.S.A. he is also a conference speaker. He holds a Bachelor of Theology and Master of Theology from Evangel Christian University, and a Doctorate of Ministry from Southwest Bible College and Seminary.